THE SCARIEST PLACES ON EARTH

RMS QUEEN MARY

BY MICHAEL FERUT

BELLWETHER·MEDIA·MINNEAPOLIS, MN

Are you ready to take it to the extreme?
Torque books thrust you into the action-packed world
of sports, vehicles, mystery, and adventure. These
books may include dirt, smoke, fire, and chilling tales.
WARNING : read at your own risk.

Library of Congress Cataloging-in-Publication Data

Ferut, Michael, author.
  RMS Queen Mary / by Michael Ferut.
    pages cm. -- (Torque. The Scariest Places on Earth)
  Summary: "Engaging images accompany information about the RMS Queen Mary. The combination
of high-interest subject matter and light text is intended for students in grades 3 through 7"-- Provided by
publisher.
  Audience: Ages 7-12.
  Audience: Grades 3 to 7.
  Includes bibliographical references and index.
  ISBN 978-1-60014-996-2 (hardcover : alk. paper)
  1. Queen Mary (Steamship)--Juvenile literature. 2. Ghosts--Juvenile literature. I. Title. II. Series: Scariest
places on earth. III. Series: Torque (Minneapolis, Minn.)
  BF1486.F47 2014
  133.1'29--dc23
                                    2014002070

This edition first published in 2015 by Bellwether Media, Inc.

Printed in the United States of America, North Mankato, MN.

TABLE OF CONTENTS

ABOARD THE QUEEN MARY.............................4

A STORIED SHIP 8

FLOATING GHOSTS? 12

GLOSSARY 22

TO LEARN MORE 23

INDEX...24

CHAPTER 1

ABOARD THE QUEEN MARY

It is your first night in the hotel aboard the *Queen Mary*. A strange tapping wakes you up. Could it be a hotel worker? You open the door. But nobody is there.

You go back to bed. Suddenly, the lights flash on and the bathroom faucet starts running. You jump up to turn the water off. You look around. Nobody else is in the room. Who is keeping you awake?

CHAPTER 2

A STORIED SHIP

RMS *Queen Mary* was built in Clydebank, Scotland to be a large passenger ship. Its first voyage was in 1936. The ship was known for luxury. It carried the rich and famous from Britain to New York.

During World War II, the U.S. and British militaries needed the *Queen Mary's* size and speed. They used it to carry soldiers around the world.

GHOST RIDE

The military painted the *Queen Mary* gray. They called it "The Gray Ghost." Even though it was big, the ship snuck around without being seen.

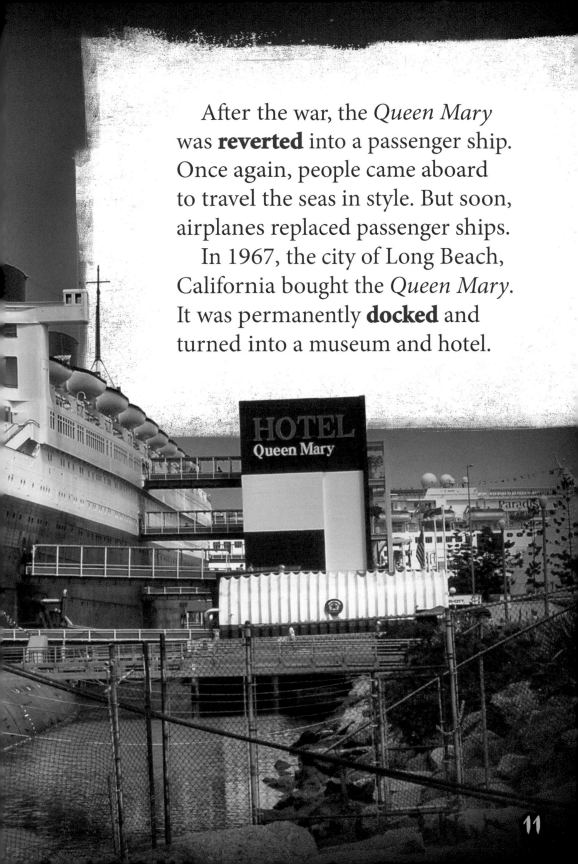

After the war, the *Queen Mary* was **reverted** into a passenger ship. Once again, people came aboard to travel the seas in style. But soon, airplanes replaced passenger ships.

In 1967, the city of Long Beach, California bought the *Queen Mary*. It was permanently **docked** and turned into a museum and hotel.

CHAPTER 3

FLOATING GHOSTS?

Soon after the hotel opened, guests and workers started having odd experiences. Some heard creepy tapping noises on the pipes and walls. Others reported seeing ghostly figures wearing outdated clothing styles.

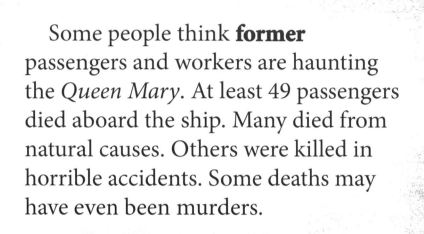

Some people think **former** passengers and workers are haunting the *Queen Mary*. At least 49 passengers died aboard the ship. Many died from natural causes. Others were killed in horrible accidents. Some deaths may have even been murders.

TRAP DOOR

The ghost of John Pedder is said to haunt the ship. He worked in the *Queen Mary's* engine room. During a drill, he was trapped under a heavy door and crushed to death. He is the most commonly seen ghost on the *Queen Mary*.

During World War II, the *Queen Mary* **collided** with a smaller British ship. The smaller ship was destroyed and its crew was **stranded**. More than 300 men drowned.

Many years later, people heard odd noises on the *Queen Mary* where it hit the other ship. Today, people still report the sounds of a loud crash, rushing water, and pounding on the walls.

JOHN S. SMITH

A CREEPY KITCHEN

A military cook may have been murdered on the ship. It is said he was pushed into an oven by angry soldiers. Some visitors say they can hear his screams.

Today, many hotel guests visit the empty first-class swimming pool. The pool area is said to be among the ship's most haunted places.

Guests have reported seeing a ghostly woman diving into thin air. Others have heard little girls splashing and playing. Even though it has no water, wet footprints appear around the pool.

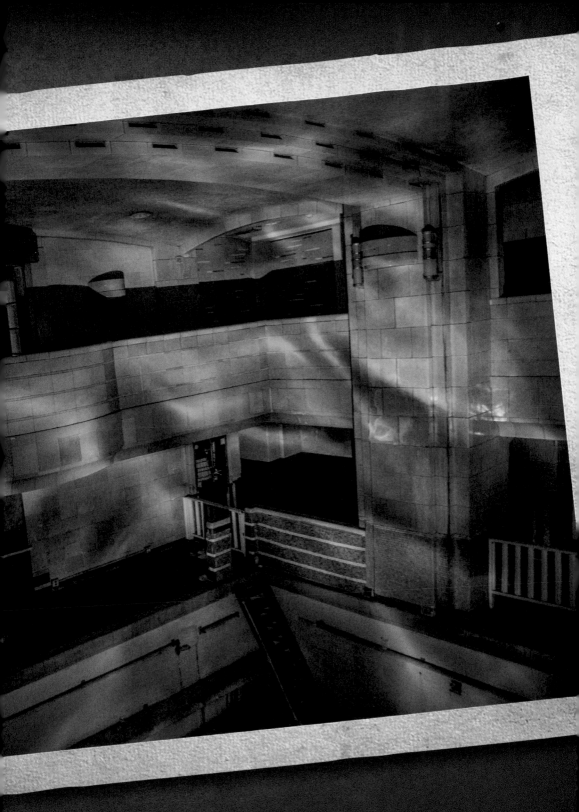

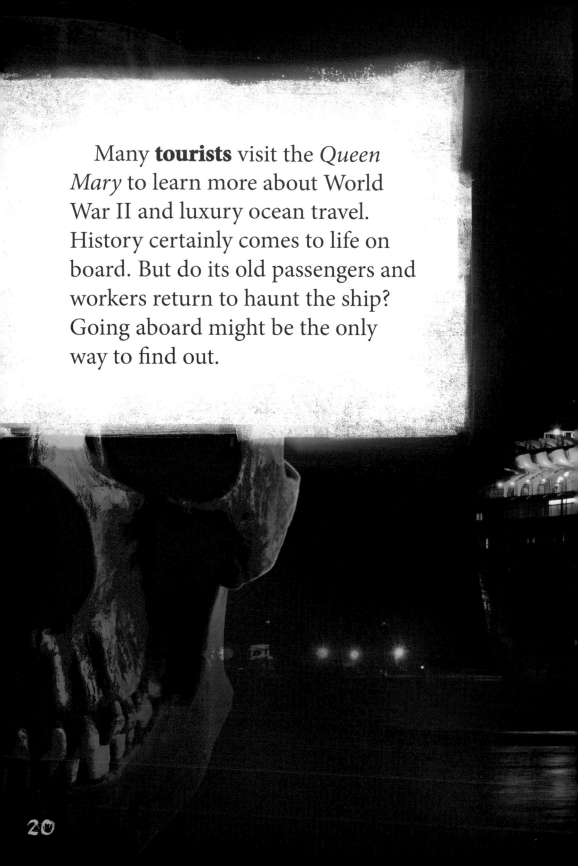

Many **tourists** visit the *Queen Mary* to learn more about World War II and luxury ocean travel. History certainly comes to life on board. But do its old passengers and workers return to haunt the ship? Going aboard might be the only way to find out.

GLOSSARY

collided—crashed into something or someone

docked—parked in a harbor

former—from the past

luxury—something that is nicer than you really need

outdated—old or from a past time period

reverted—changed back

stranded—left behind

tourists—people who travel to visit another place

voyage—a trip or journey

TO LEARN MORE

AT THE LIBRARY

Chandler, Matt. *The World's Most Haunted Places*. Mankato, Minn.: Capstone Press, 2012.

Parvis, Sarah E. *Haunted Hotels*. New York, N.Y.: Bearport Pub., 2008.

Shea, Therese. *Haunted! The Queen Mary*. New York, N.Y.: Gareth Stevens Publishing, 2013.

ON THE WEB

Learning more about the RMS *Queen Mary* is as easy as 1, 2, 3.

1. Go to www.factsurfer.com.

2. Enter "RMS Queen Mary" into the search box.

3. Click the "Surf" button and you will see a list of related web sites.

With factsurfer.com, finding more information is just a click away.

INDEX

airplanes, 11
Britain, 8, 17
Clydebank, Scotland, 8
collided, 17
cook, 17
deaths, 14, 15
faucet, 7
ghost, 12, 15, 18
Gray Ghost, The, 8
guests, 12, 18
hotel, 4, 11, 12, 18
lights, 7
Long Beach, California, 11
luxury, 8, 20
military, 8, 17
museum, 11
New York, 8
noises, 12, 17
passenger ship, 8, 11
Pedder, John, 15

pipes, 12
soldiers, 8, 17
swimming pool, 18
tapping, 4, 12
tourists, 17, 20
United States, 8
voyage, 8
worker, 4, 12, 14, 20
World War II, 8, 11, 17, 20